Scotland in colour

Introduction and commentaries by
Alastair Inglis Dunnett

B. T. BATSFORD LTD LONDON

First published 1970

© B. T. Batsford Ltd 1970

Filmset in Great Britain by Filmtype Services Ltd, Scarborough, Yorkshire

Made and printed in Denmark by F. E. Bording Ltd, Copenhagen
for the publishers B. T. Batsford Ltd, 4 Fitzhardinge Street, London W1

7134 0019 6

Contents

Introduction

Scotland in Colour. To many that means, and rightly, the richness of tartan which has long since been known all over the world. So let us start with what is perhaps the most glamorous wear for men yet to be invented.

The kilt is to be seen at its most dynamic at affairs like the Braemar Highland Games where athletes compete with one another, most spectacularly in the field events. Tossing the caber, a young giant of a tree with the branches stripped from its trunk, is a sport unique to these occasions and even the air seems to hold its breath as the Gathering waits to see whether the attempt will be successful or not. And then there is hammer throwing. As the competitor birls round and round before loosing the heavy hammer on its soaring way to plunge into the ground with a heavy dunt many yards away, the kilt beneath his singlet whirls with all the flash of a passing kingfisher and then gradually comes to rest around the muscled thighs.

The kilt can be seen to quite as great effect though in somewhat gentler form at dances and in the performances of the increasing number of groups who have over the last twenty years been contributing to the resurgence of Scottish folk music and country dancing. There is nothing more pleasing to see: the gentle flow of colours as the gentlemen in their full highland dress tartan mingle with the ladies in their white flowing evening gowns, brightened with the tartan plaids worn diagonally across one shoulder and fastened with a Cairngorm brooch.

To many, however, the kilt is best to be appreciated worn military style at the Tattoo staged yearly on the Esplanade of Edinburgh Castle under floodlights in late August and September. This is an event which happily overlaps the Edinburgh International Festival of Music and Drama. There is something in the splendour of this sight accompanied by the sound of the pipes and drums of the Highland regiments which brings out the atavistic in every Scot present, which makes the heart of the exile, returned for a brief visit, to beat with a painful sweetness; and which gives the foreigner seeing such a spectacle for the first time a sense of awe and of being privileged to take part in a tribal mystery which comes near to laying bare the heart of the nation.

It is, however, seldom that Scots wear the kilt for every day dress. It is hard to analyse why this should be so for it is a garment cool in the summer when the gentle breezes can waft it in a seemly way round the thighs and warm in winter when the more stormy blasts beat the solid material against the legs and keep the cold out. Of course the kilt is Highland wear and there is a deep-rooted abhorrence among most Scots to seeing it being worn daily outside the Highlands except on special occasions like those which have already been mentioned.

In any case quite as popular as the kilt is tweed and most Scots, men or women, have at least one article of tweed in their wardrobes.

Ah! The subtlety of tweed. It comes in many weights and colours. It may be the finest most discreet check for elegant wear in town and city or frankly hairy for the country and the hills. In colour it may be sombre, fit for the Kirk; or a heather mixture where peat brown mingles with purple, red and other finely shaded rural tints; or it may be the blue of a sparrow's egg, a reminder of the skies of the Western Isles where the tweed is fashioned.

If this should be thought to be pure romancing then a visit to one of the many clothing stores in Scotland's cities should quickly dispel the accusation. Let the visitor ask to be shown a variety of bolts of tweed. As length after length of cloth snakes out along the counter, only the most stolid will not find in the inner eye a kaleidoscope of colour forming, dissolving and reforming in the most subtle patterns.

Subtle! That word again. Yet it is apt. The plain colours of the simple Scottish tweeds, the blend of the mixtures, reveal to those with eyes to see, the very heart of the matter concerning the countryside and the people of Scotland. Tweed in the first instance was made from wool gathered from sheep, nurtured by Scottish shepherds on the hills, and spun and woven by their wives in the crofts of the Highlands and the cottages in the Borders in the south of the country. The colours came from the dyes that were naturally available and so reflected the countryside in which particular tweeds were produced. And there was yet another way in which the surrounding countryside made its influence felt.

The creative eye of the artist cannot escape the environment in which he lives and works, no matter how what he receives is later modified and developed. The genius of the early tweed makers was reflected in the colour patterns evoked by the changing seasons and the moods of the seas, rivers, lochs and the land around them as well as the constant shift of light in the skies above. The elemental bare grey black mountains of Assynt, the peat moors, the heather, the pastels of pastureland, the chartreuse green of summer seas lapping silver white beaches, the autumn tints of trees by Border streams; all these influences and many more have worked on and challenged the creative minds of the artists who have fashioned Scottish tweed. It has been an abiding challenge. Even now, when hand-woven tweed is a rarity and most of the cloth is produced in mills, the designers employed there draw upon the old traditions for inspiration for their patterns and still try to capture what must always escape even the greatest creative ability.

Modern photographers with their vastly improved colour techniques, come very near to catching the fleeting moment, but even the greatest of them will admit that techniques are by no means perfect and recount agonies of having for one reason or another missed the perfect colour study. Their frustrations are greater than any angler bemoaning the big salmon that got away in one of Scotland's great rivers like the Dee in Aberdeenshire or the Tweed in the south.

Yet even a casual glance at the illustrations in this book will show how very near photographers can come to perfection. A longer, deeper look at the sequence of photographs, supplemented by the narrative which accompanies them will, it is hoped, evoke a feel for the Scottish countryside and for the people who live and work there.

This is not to claim that all aspects of Scottish life are covered. The aim is at once to remind Scots of the richness of their heritage and to give an opportunity to the stranger of glimpsing something at least of what

Scotland has to offer.

It is surprising how parochial native-born Scots can be when it comes to their own country. Even in days of speedy road and air transport many Lowland Scots have never penetrated beyond Inverness. Glasgow people tend to spend their holidays in the Western Highlands and Edinburgh folk in the North East, Fife or the Borders. In an astonishing number of cases they return to the same area, even the same resort, year after year. Their holiday patch becomes, as it were, their home from home. As the most densely populated part of Scotland lies in the centre industrial belt stretching across the waist of the country from Glasgow to Edinburgh most Scots know this region well and there is little point in mirroring it here. There is point, however, in covering a wide canvas outside this area and if home Scots make some new discoveries it is all to the good. If they be incensed that some favourite spot be not mentioned then let it be a matter for them to air with their acquaintance. Such a dialogue cannot but shake folk out of ruts and lead to new voyages of discovery in their own land.

The stranger on the brink of a voyage into Scotland is unlikely to be enamoured of glowing accounts and illustrations of industrial achievement, activities which are confined to a comparatively small area of the country's land mass. We are, in any event, as a nation not slow to inform visitors of our prowess in industrial and other accomplishments. If they be interested they can easily fit into their itinerary a visit to one of the Clyde shipyards, to the oil complex round Grangemouth, to the new collieries, the nuclear power stations, the rapidly developing electronics industry in some areas. In Fife, for example, the old shaky dependence on the one-industry economy of coal is fast giving way to a more diverse way of life, concentrating not only on introducing electronic and other light industries, but also providing large recreation parks with facilities for golfing, yachting, hill walking and the like.

Visitors can, if they wish, gain a broad picture of the many exciting new developments in Scotland by visiting the offices of the Scottish Council (Development and Industry) on their way through Edinburgh. They can hear of plans to bring renewed vitality to industry in the Clyde

Estuary and of opposition to them from, among others, salmon fishers and lovers of scenery and wild life; of equally controversial plans to bring new work to depopulated areas like the Borders and Galloway in the south. In Inverness they will find that the Highlands and Islands Development Board is actively encouraging the growth of small and large industries in an area of the country long noted for its scenic beauty, but not for its capacity to provide work for the people living there. They can learn if they will, and perhaps with amazement, of the grants, loans and subsidies which may be made available for such projects—projects which may vary in size from a small fly-tying business to supply trout and salmon fishers, to the setting up of a large international petrochemical complex on the shores of the Moray Firth and the establishment there of a new town of tens of thousands of people.

All this visitors may easily care to do as they journey through Scotland. Yet it would not be courteous or even effective to deave them with details of the workaday life of the country before they have even started their journey. Better by far that an awareness of all that Scotland has to offer should creep up on them from the beguiling influence of the countryside and the many conversations they will have with the Scots they meet on their way.

It is with this in mind that the illustrations have been arranged in a sequence suitable for a wayfarer through Scotland entering by one of the eastern approaches, travelling through the eastern borders to the capital city of Edinburgh, thence up the east coast to Aberdeen, across the country to Inverness and the north, down the west coast with forays into the central Highlands; and so to the south west and Galloway and out by the western approaches to England through Dumfries. There are brief visits to Skye and the Outer Hebridean island of Harris. But travellers wishing to explore the Inner and Outer Hebrides satisfactorily would need more than one journey to accomplish their end. More than one voyager has arrived at an island for a week-end, stayed for weeks, even months and in rare cases for a lifetime.

Now one general point about Scotland before the journey begins. It looks a small country on the map of the world and indeed it has just over five million inhabitants, but geographically it can be bewildering. Even our closest neighbours, the English, are sometimes misled.

A broadcasting man in Glasgow was once startled by a voice from his London office asking him at 11 o'clock in the morning to "Nip up to Wick" and bring back a tape recording for a news magazine programme to be broadcast from London at seven o'clock that evening. "Impossible", he said when he got his breath back, and was at once suspected of laziness, dereliction of duty, if not total insubordination, until he pointed out that Wick was several hundred miles from Glasgow and that, even if he could get the interview required, he could not possibly in the time go to Wick and back unless perchance he chartered a special 'plane. Even then . . . but that was the end of the conversation.

That London editor is by no means the only Englishman to believe that all parts of Scotland are within a stone's throw of either Edinburgh or Glasgow. Overseas visitors from the Prairies of Canada or the United States or the Back Blocks of Australia who think nothing of motoring 200 miles or more to and from a dinner engagement or dance find that the geography of Scotland does not lend itself easily to such practices except along the few first-class main roads. And Scotland is a surprisingly diverse country about which it is fatal to generalise.

It is fashionable and perhaps convenient to divide Scotland into two broad regions known as the Highlands and the Lowlands. The city of Perth in central Scotland often likes to be known as "the gateway to the Highlands" and certainly there is some very lovely Highland country to the north and west of Perth. To the north and east of Perth, however, there is some excellent lowland arable country. Conversely in the Lowlands of Scotland in the very south of the country, in the Borders, there are a number of very barren heather-clad hills which are distinctly Highland in character. Some in despair have tried to draw a Highland line on a rule of thumb basis up the Great Glen from Fort William to Inverness, a stretch that includes Loch Ness and the Monster. North west of that line, they say, everything is Highland but they also have to add very hurriedly that to the east they must include the Grampians and to the south the large County of Argyll and many off-shore islands which are indubitably Highland in geography and cultural tradition. Still smarting at the refusal of the country to be meekly divided into two parts they have to admit that to the north east of Inverness is the Black Isle, a low-lying peninsula so called because of its black soil or its comparative freedom from snow. The Black Isle is one of the most fertile lowland districts of Scotland. Worse still in the top north-east corner of the country lies Caithness, bleak indeed but a vast lowland plain where a mound of thirty feet can assume the status of a hill and in some instances give a view for as many miles around.

All this being admitted, it is not even true to say that all the land in the Highlands is made up of lofty mountains and lochs and is a pretty savage and uncomfortable area in which to live in the winter time. For owing to the Gulf Stream parts of north-western Scotland enjoy a sub-tropical climate where palm trees flourish.

This is not meant to confuse. Rather the aim is to show that Scotland is a country which within a remarkably small area of land can offer the pleasures of the gentler Lowlands almost cheek by jowl with majestic hill country.

The traveller who stands at Carter Bar, the boundary between Scotland and England on the inland approach by the east coast and winds his way down the steep hillside to Jedburgh is made immediately aware of this paradox. He is officially in the Lowlands but at first the land around him is obviously fit for grazing nothing but sheep. Then comes cattle country and if after his descent he ventures east into Berwickshire and the Merse land, he will find strong soil capable of producing many tons of barley to the acre. To reach Edinburgh he will again have to pass through rugged hill country before he sees the great plain of the Lothians spread out before him and realises that this is one of the most fertile areas in the world.

He will have other adjustments to make for the language of Scotland, although officially English and spoken normally with clarity and due attention to the claims of vowels and consonants, has many dialects and each and every one of them reflect the history of the areas concerned.

Not all Scotsmen are capable of understanding each other. The great cultural division in language is between Gaelic, related to Welsh, Irish and the patois of Britanny in France, and English. Gaelic is spoken mainly in the north and Western Highlands and is not only a language but the oral expression of a whole culture. Few Lowland Scots speak it but through radio and television it is now being learned and appreciated by an increasing number of people. Were it not for the efforts of these mass media Gaelic would in the earlier part of this century have been in grave danger of dying out, although it is scarcely conceivable that the rich heritage of Gaelic music either sung, in some cases as an altogether distinctive form of mouth music without words, or played on the bag-pipes in the form of the more popular pipe tunes or the classic severity of the Great Pibroch, could ever die.

Another quite distinctive language and musical tradition is to be found in Shetland which until the thirteenth century belonged to Nor-way and not to Scotland. There the language is neither Scots nor Norse and is certainly very much harsher than Gaelic though the music and songs have a lilting beauty of their own. Even in the Lowlands the speech of a man from the Buchan districts of north-east Scotland, where the Doric is spoken and owes a good deal to the Low Countries of Europe with which the area once conducted a flourishing trade, would be unintelligible to those in other parts of Scotland. Many Glaswegians speak a dialect of English which they may claim to be international because it can be heard in so many of the world's ports but which makes the citizens of Edinburgh shudder. In fairness, it may be said that the Glaswegians are as uncomfortably affected by the harder clipped accents of the Capital.

The very diversity of accents and dialects all over Scotland gives the spoken word a fullness. Sometimes a phrase passed hurriedly at a moment of crisis comes very near to poetry. A grieve, that is a farm foreman, came rushing up to the farmer one sultry summer day when everyone was working against time and impending rain to get the crop in from a field in the north of Fife. He stood for a moment catching his breath and then, with the classic simplicity of a herald pronouncing doom in a Greek Tragedy proclaimed "The flichts o' the binder is broke". This being translated literally to "The flights of the binder are broken" corrects the grammar, descends to bathos and shatters the sense of tragedy hanging over that harvest field; for without the reaper and binder the crop would have to remain at risk to the weather.

Robert Burns had no need to create the living texture of his Scottish verse out of a vacuum. It was in being all around him waiting to be caught and held by his genius. Scots poets writing today tap the same reservoir. Like Burns they are bi-lingual. They can write in standard English as well as Scots.

This bi-lingualism is common in Scotland and may be reassuring to overseas visitors worried by possible difficulty in understanding the profusion of tongues around them. The Scot working or relaxing among his fellows will naturally use the spoken word of his surroundings and our vocabulary would be a great deal poorer if he did not. But when strangers are present he can and does speak a standard English coloured interestingly by accent or inflection but understandable throughout the English-speaking world. There is no surrender of pride in national or regional identity in this. It is simply a matter of courtesy.

The most telling way to hear the interplay of sounds that go to make up spoken Scots is to mingle with the crowds attending the Show of the Royal Highland and Agricultural Society of Scotland, held every year at Ingliston just outside Edinburgh in the third week of June. For to "The Highland" come country folk from all over to see and judge for themselves the best livestock and the most useful new developments in agricultural machinery. On the showground they mingle with the men who make, service and sell the machines and with "boffins" working on new ideas to increase farm production and lower costs.

At night there are high jinks and *ceilidhs*—highland song-feasts which may be either highly formal or wildly informal depending on the occasion, the mood and sometimes, one must admit, the amount of whisky consumed.

Whisky! An emotive word to the Scot if ever there was one. A good servant and a bad master, so they say. Like most of the good things in life, it has its dangers but used properly it does make glad the heart of man. You run down the quality of a good malt whisky to a knowledge-able Scot with the same measure of impunity you would expect if you insulted a rare wine in the presence of the head of a French family which has been producing great wines for centuries.

In a more utilitarian sense, whisky can help to keep out the bitter cold of the winter's day from a shepherd striding the high hills to check his flock; or from the studmaster and his fellows attending the sales of pedigree bulls in Perth in the first two weeks of February every year. The potent blood of Scottish livestock reaches to many countries and sales of Aberdeen Angus and Scotch Shorthorn beef breeds attract among others hard-headed businessmen with interests in the pampas of Argentina or the cattle-raising lands of North America, Australasia and Africa. Pedigree bull sales in the dairying country of the South West in Ayrshire and Galloway attract a similar interest and so do the Galloway beef cattle. "Belted" in Galloway does not refer to an earl but to a breed of the indigenous black, dun, brown beef cattle which carry a broad white belt behind their shoulders.

A deal closed with a handshake and a dram of whisky may well later be cemented by that most Scottish of rituals, a high tea. To the southern English this is an appalling conglomeration of mutually indigestible comestibles. To many Scots it is what naturally occurs around six o'clock of an evening and crowns the day. It enticingly presents such native delicacies as minced beef topped with an egg, finnan haddock ditto, a variety of cold meats, soda scones, drop scones, potato scones, treacle scones *et alia;* cakes which entrance the eye and enhance the stomach in a way to make choleric our diet-fad conscious doctors; all washed down with torrents of well-masked tea brewed from mixtures of the Chinese and Indian varieties of the plant, mixtures which are fre-quently handed down with some degree of secrecy from generation to generation. Gastronomically, high tea is Scotland's secret weapon shed-ding a fall-out of beatific somnolence on its *aficionados*.

Fish frequently figure in the place of honour at these orgies and the smoked haddocks, kippered herrings or fresh herrings in oatmeal are a reminder of the hard men who fish from the ports of large cities like Aberdeen, the smaller havens of the Clyde Estuary, the East Neuk of Fife or the rocky inlets of the Buchan coast and the townships of the western Highlands and Islands.

A Scottish table set for a ritual high tea with visitors expected either from home or abroad is an unforgettable, colourful sight. And as it is being digested and a ritual dram of whisky taken before farewells, the traveller, however sober, may see in the amber fluid served in a glass of finely-cut Edinburgh crystal, a renewed kaleidoscope of the flashing tartans, sombre and gay tweeds, the blackness of the north-western mountains, the translucent skies of the islands in high summer; brown trout lying still in border burns, the fishing fleets reaching out into a lowering North Sea; and hear the Babel sounds of a myriad Scottish voices; the sight . . . the sound . . . the feel . . . the experience of Scotland in Colour.

MELROSE ABBEY

Melrose Abbey lies under the triple summits of the Eildon Hills which dominate the low lying Border countryside around them as the road winds down from Carter Bar. The crops and the livestocks and the grazings must have gladdened the eyes of English border reivers. Their arrival caused the alarm to be raised from watchtower to watchtower—peels they are called and can still be seen—so that the men of the Scottish border burghs might stand to arms. The superstitious might shudder as they passed the Eildons for fear that the spirit of Michael Scot the famed Scottish warlock be upon them. It was his power, so it was said, that summoned the devil to cleave the summits of the Eildon Hills into three peaks with two mighty blows. Drowsing by the banks of a Border stream it is not difficult to appreciate how some anonymous author wrote of Thomas the Rhymer being enchanted into the service of the Queen of Fairyland and going through hell and high water for her.

In such a land the church may well have felt it best to have a strong representation. There is a cluster of abbeys at Jedburgh, Melrose, Dryburgh and Kelso. The farming skills of the monks are continued by modern border farmers and the Kelso Ram Sales held every year in the first week of September are world famous, particularly among breeders of Border Leicesters, and Oxford and Suffolk Downs.

The twentieth-century secular religion of the area is rugby football and many a touring team has suffered its first reverse in Britain on a Border ground. It is a stirring, even aesthetic sight to see the final of a seven-a-side rugby tournament played out in late evening spring sunshine on the famous Greenyards pitch at Melrose with the coloured jerseys vivid against the backdrop of the Eildon Hills.

THE PEEBLESHIRE HILLS

The Peebleshire countryside which links the southern borders to Edinburgh and the Lothians accepts as her own the fishermen and the hill walker, the lover of solitude and of quiet pleasant places. It inspired much of the work and way of thinking of John Buchan as well as plots for his early writing. The names of some of the characters in his novels, like Lamancha are taken from place names in the area. He chose Tweedsmuir as his title when he was made a peer from the name of the Peebleshire parish. And Tweedsmuir is a reminder that this is the area where the river Tweed rises in a mere trickle to start on its journey to the sea at Berwick-upon-Tweed.

The hills in the background are well suited to the needs of that hardiest of sheep breeds, the Scottish Blackface and their wool is woven into the design of many a carpet. Where farming is not economic, the Forestry Commission has established plantations. The trees at various stages of development add a landscaping quality and additional colour to the countryside.

TRAQUAIR HOUSE

Traquair House is one of the oldest in Scotland. It is believed that the early parts were used as a hunting lodge as far back as the Middle Ages. Its main gates have never been opened since the late eighteenth century. One romantic but not entirely authenticated explanation is that the gates were shut after the young Pretender had paid a visit to the Earl of Traquair in 1745. Moved by loyalty and devotion the Earl declared that those gates should never again be opened till the Stuarts enjoyed their own again.

Another story has it that they were ordained to remain closed by the seventh Earl of Traquair after the death of his wife, until there was another Countess of Traquair to enter them. His heir died unmarried and there never has been another Countess.

The present owner of the house, Mr. Maxwell Stuart, keeps it open to the public and there is a private chapel and many fine pieces of eighteenth-century furniture among its treasures.

Mr. Stuart also brews a notable Scottish ale which sends visitors on their way suitably refreshed.

THE PENTLAND HILLS

Almost within the city boundaries of Edinburgh lie the Pentland Hills which have always been a favourite courting ground for the young. They are a joy to walkers, who, thanks to the numerous and jealously guarded "rights of way", can move about freely. Many of the walks are efficiently but unobtrusively sign-posted. At Woodhouselea there is a Pony Trekking Centre with Icelandic ponies on which it is possible to range the hills far and wide. On the northern slopes an artificial ski run gives training facilities for those who wish later to progress to the natural snow slopes of the Cairngorms or Glencoe.

Robert Louis Stevenson was fascinated by the Pentlands and an old manse in their shadow was the setting for his fearsome long-short story "Thrawn Janet". The Pentlands hold the main reservoirs which supply Edinburgh with water. In hard winters these reservoirs, like Threipmuir are natural skating arenas. Beneath and on the lower slopes there are several well-patronised golf courses, where the game may be enjoyed with fine views of both sea and landscapes at a fraction of the cost such facilities could command in the south of England.

SWANSTON COTTAGE

Also in the Pentlands lies Swanston Cottage where Robert Louis Stevenson lived for some time as a youth. The city fathers of Edinburgh have never been averse to a degree of merry making, provided in the nineteenth century at least it was done discreetly. Earlier ages were less fastidious. Swanston however provided the magistrates with a venue which was charming, conveniently near and sufficiently removed from prying eyes.

Times have now changed. The Town Council still owns the village and deserves great credit for having restored the cottages with their attractive thatched roofs. To become a tenant there is faintly like being able to pass, like the scriptural camel, through the eye of a needle. There are so many restrictions; and to be fair so many applicants. Swanston Village is a charming sight, but no longer boisterous. There is not an inn in sight.

Where the magistrates now do their roystering is their own business. Those who wish to find pleasant Pentland inns would do well to concentrate on the southern side of the hills where they will find several notable hostelries like Habbie's Howe at Nine-mile-burn with its famous association with the poet Allan Ramsay.

EDINBURGH

This is the most European skyline in Great Britain. Edinburgh the capital of Scotland could never by any stretch of the imagination be mistaken for an English city. On the left the spine of the Old Town rises to its peak on the Castle Rock. In the centre the clock tower of the Station Hotel and further along the Gothic pinnacles of the Scott Monument mark the line of the world-famous boulevard of Princes Street and also the boundary between the Old and New Towns.

The monument in the foreground is to Dugald Stewart, a progressive professor of Edinburgh University in the early nineteenth century, much interested in the development of the New Town. Some of his more social moments were spent attending meetings of the Friday Club established in 1803, enjoying its conviviality along with such luminaries as Sydney Smith and Walter Scott. They believed in doing themselves well, were great claret drinkers and by the 1820s their dinners were costing the then astronomic sum of £2 or more a head.

Today Edinburgh has a flourishing school of young architects of undoubted ability and many of them of similar tastes although perhaps not on the same lavish scale. They mingle with artists, writers, poets and musicians as well as with craftsmen, scientists and technologists in the classless pubs, clubs and eating houses which abound in Edinburgh and indeed all over Scotland.

The skyline of the Old Town of Edinburgh has a welcome look of unshakeable permanence but even within it and certainly all around new buildings are going up and the old being restored. In ways of thought new or re-heated ideas are sustaining the warmth that has always existed behind the apparently cold exterior of grey stone.

DUGALD STEWART
BORN NOVEMBER 22 1753
DIED JUNE 11 1828

HOLYROODHOUSE

The palace of Holyroodhouse is austerely bleak. It is so seldom used as a dwelling place that it achieves the air of a somewhat empty museum. One of its most interesting features is the fountain in the courtyard, which however is a copy of an original to be found in the main courtyard of the ancient palace of Scotland's kings built in the fifteenth and sixteenth centuries at Linlithgow. This fountain was designed and built by Flemish craftsmen, a fact which is reflected in the stone figures dressed in the period costumes of Continental workmen, but not that worn by their contemporaries in Scotland. This original fountain at Linlithgow some sixteen miles west of Edinburgh is well worth a visit.

The Abbey of Holyrood was founded in 1128 by David the First after a fortunate escape from a hunting accident but the ruins now standing are of a much later date. The present palace was built to the orders of Charles II. The architect was Sir William Bruce and the work was overseen by Robert Mylne the King's master mason.

It must have been a labour of love or political expediency rather than of practical purpose, for Charles II never visited the finished building and no sovereign after his day came near it until 1822. The palace is now used during the infrequent visits of royalty to Edinburgh and as a residence for the monarch's representative, the Lord High Commissioner, during the annual meetings of the General Assembly of the Church of Scotland in the third and fourth weeks of May.

THE BASS ROCK

The Bass Rock is a famous landmark in the Firth of Forth opposite the bracing holiday town of North Berwick which lies some sixteen miles east along the coast road from Edinburgh. Also nearby is Gullane with its famous golf courses.

The Bass is a strong natural fortress and was held as such for many months by a handful of men for James II against the forces of William of Orange. There are several accounts extant of the ploys to which the garrison were reduced to run the blockade so that they could get food and ammunition and other supplies as well as news from their many sympathisers on the mainland. Eventually after giving an honourable account of themselves the blockade of the English fleet forced their surrender. The Bass is also a famous happy hunting ground for ornithologists. Almost opposite on the mainland is the stronghold of Tantallon Castle with such a strong tactical position on a rocky promontory that although it was beseiged often during the age of gunpowder it did not fall to a bombardment until as late as 1651. Then Cromwell's artillery under General Monk smashed a way through after two days constant fire. Inland is the rich farming country of East Lothian with many charming villages among which Gifford is particularly worth a visit.

FORTH ROAD BRIDGE

The opening of the Forth Road Bridge in 1964 by the Queen, not only put the ferry out of business after a term of usefulness stretching back for well over a thousand years, it also seriously affected the passenger and carrying trade of the railway bridge.

On the other hand it opened up Fife still more to the cars of tourists and businessmen and to the commercial vehicles which were needed to bring in raw materials for Fife's rapidly expanding electronic and light industries. Over the bridge pass the finished products for re-distribution through the Port of Leith, the railway centres, or if compact and light enough, the Civil Airport at Turnhouse.

Aesthetically the two bridges seen together from the promenade at South Queensferry are a delightful contrast in style. In Europe the road bridge is only exceeded in length for single span construction by one over the Tagus in Portugal. Of its kind the railway bridge has never been equalled anywhere in the world.

DUNFERMLINE ABBEY AND PALACE

Dunfermline, a city "set upon a hill", has a commanding position on the slopes of the hills of south west Fife overlooking the Firth of Forth. One of its best known associations is that of the old Scots ballad of Sir Patrick Spens:

> *The King sat in Dunfermline Toon,*
> *Drinking the bluid-red wine,*
> *Oh who will find me a skeely skipper,*
> *To sail this ship of mine?*

A disastrous journey to Norway was the result in which the king's ship was lost with all hands on the return passage. It seems to have been top-heavy with courtiers and after its loss Dunfermline must have been an empty town.

The foundation of the Abbey goes back to the days of Malcolm Canmore. He moved the principal seat of his court to Dunfermline from further north in the eleventh century. The foundations of the eleventh century church can still be seen and there is an inspiring Romanesque nave which holds the tomb of Robert the Bruce and other Scottish kings including Malcolm Canmore.

The walls of the Palace are still standing. Hard by both Abbey and Palace is Pittencrieff Glen, the gift of the American steel multi-million-aire Andrew Carnegie who was born in Dunfermline and never forgot his birthplace. His benefactions also included free libraries throughout the length and breadth of Scotland and scholarships without which many a poor but able Scottish student would never have been able to attend a course at a university.

Peacocks are bred for sale in Pittencrieff Park, and there is a long waiting list of eager buyers.

CRAIL

Crail is one of the group of fishing ports that line the coast of the East Neuk of Fife, that eastern corner of the county jutting out into the North Sea. There used to be a flourishing trade with the Low Countries between Crail and such other small Fife havens as Elie, Pittenweem and Anstruther. Now the fishing industry is in decline and prosperity depends largely on holidaymakers. There are some splendid seaside golf courses which tend to be overshadowed by the more famous links at St. Andrews only a few miles away. The East Neuk towns are favourites with artists who appreciate the clear light air and the clean cut lines of the fishermen's churches and other buildings.

With the opening of the Forth and Tay road bridges people working in Edinburgh and Dundee have found this part of Fife an attractive and convenient place in which to live.

STONEHAVEN

The route from Fife to Stonehaven has been made much speedier by the opening of the Tay Road Bridge which leads straight into the heart of Dundee. This city once renowned for the whaling trade and still famous as the centre of the jute industry is also the place where a certain Mrs Keiller discovered how to make orange marmalade. This was the start of a flourishing jam trade largely supplied by the nearby soft growing area in and around the Carse of Gowrie.

Angus and Kincardine are very fertile with great crops of oats, barley and wheat as well as sugar beet and thriving livestock.

Like the coastal towns of Fife, Stonehaven has come to depend more and more on holidaymakers and the pleasure craft in the harbour outnumber the fishing boats. The style of the building around the harbour, however, is a reminder that this too was once a flourishing fishing port.

It is a short fast run up the coast from Stonehaven to Aberdeen. Inland the "Slug" road crosses to Banchory on Royal Deeside.

BALMORAL CASTLE AND LOCHNAGAR

Royal Deeside with its fine views of the Grampians is a splendid example of how Lowland and Highland country exist cheek by jowl in Scotland. The snow-covered slopes of Lochnagar contrast with the parkland surrounding Balmoral Castle.

This is one of the best-known parts of Scotland, particularly overseas. It would be attractive in any event because of its natural beauty. Its world-wide fame, however, is comparatively modern and was established by Queen Victoria's devotion to Balmoral Castle built in the mid-fifties of the nineteenth century on an estate bought in 1847 by the Prince consort, who was himself largely responsible for the design.

Nearby is Crathie Church which is still attended by the Queen and other members of the royal family when they are in residence at Balmoral. It is more modern still for the foundation stone was laid by Queen Victoria in 1893.

Further up Deeside and almost surrounded by mountains is Braemar where the famous Highland Gathering is held every year in September.

MACDUFF

Macduff is one of the fishing ports that are sited round the coast from Aberdeen along the estuary of the Moray Firth. This is an important area for the herring fishing industry. Although some boats still sail from the smaller ports many of the fishermen prefer to live in places like Macduff and fish out of the larger towns where facilities are better. Peterhead and Fraserburgh, for instance, have quick-freezing plants and canning factories. At Fraserburgh there is also a meat and oil factory.

The weather in the area is mostly dry and sunny and this, combined with sandy beaches and sheltered coves, makes it attractive to holiday-makers.

Inland and particularly in the valley of the Spey and its tributaries lie some of Scotland's greatest distilleries. These are a source of comfort to the pockets, if not necessarily to the palates, of a succession of Treasury ministers no matter what their politics. It is also a source of regret to many Scots to reflect how many million gallons are kept in bond there, the price being what it is.

LOCH CAIRNBAWN WITH QUINAG

The far north west of Scotland is a land where the majesty of the mountains combines with a serenity of light to create, as if by magic, an inner peace in the mind and spirit. Those who have been there appreciate that no words nor even the paintings of the late Sir D. Y. Cameron, which are very fine indeed, can quite capture its ambience.

It is old, old country. Many of the mountains rise sheer from marshy land. They are not particularly high but they gain their effect from their isolation and from the grandeur of massive slabs of rock totally devoid of vegetation. The marshes beneath them are strewn white with cotton flower and what appear as small boulders turn out, on closer examination, to be huge rocks in some cases as big as churches.

Those solitaries like Quinag (with its five peaks) and Stac Polly with its ferocious jagged pinnacles are well nigh as old as time. They belong to the upper crust of the world that, but for such as they, vanished during the Ice Ages. The most glorious is perhaps Suilven, vulgarly known as the Sugar Loaf, a classic instance of human *lèse-majesté* to the natural world.

LOCH BROOM

Loch Broom lies south of Suilven in a hilly but comparatively gentler, softer countryside. It is one of the sea lochs which strike deep into the heart of the Highlands from Scotland's west coast.

Across its mouth lie the Summer Isles warmed by the flow of the Gulf Stream. On one of them it is surprising to find a small orchard of apple trees in what is known as the Irish Garden. It is said that some enterprising Irishmen carried peat to this island in their boats as ballast which helped to establish the soil for this garden and sailed back with herring which are plentiful in these parts.

Ullapool on the north shores of Loch Broom was founded by the British Fisheries Society in 1788. Advice on its building came from the architect Robert Mylne and also from Thomas Telford, the bridge builder. The result is an attractive village of white-washed houses with clean, simple, utilitarian lines. Ullapool backs the uncertain financial stability of any herring fishing port with a flourishing tourist trade. Once "hooked", holidaymakers tend to come back to Ullapool year after year. One of the attractions lies at the south end of Loch Broom where the Falls of Measach roar over 200 feet down into the boiling waters of the narrow Corrieshalloch Gorge.

LOCH MAREE WITH SLIOCH

Slioch is another of these elemental mountains in the north west of Scotland which soar out of the surrounding countryside.

The road west along the shores of Loch Maree from Kinlochlewe, where there is a National Nature Reserve, gives spectacular views of the peaks of Torridon to the south.

At Inverewe the landscape changes abruptly from a barren to a lush beauty. On a small peninsula Osgood Mackenzie, who realised the potentials of the warmer micro-climate in this area, bought the estate of Inverewe in 1862 and began to create there the garden of his dreams. He planted trees against the great Atlantic winds and brought soil sometimes even in fishing creels, to make flower beds out of what had once been heather studded with wild berries. His work was carried on by his daughter, Mrs Mairi Sawyer until 1952 when she presented it to the National Trust for Scotland with an endowment to which the Pilgrim Trust added £10,000.

About a hundred thousand visitors go to Inverewe every year to see the palm trees and ferns, the silver birches, the Himalayan lilies and giant forget-me-nots from the South Pacific growing as if to the manner born among the heather.

CROFTERS COTTAGE IN WESTER ROSS

This winter scene is a reminder that Scotland has beauty to offer all the year round. Some travellers prefer to see the countryside when the leaves are off the trees and it is possible to achieve wider vistas as well as appreciate known views in a new light.

The plantings of the Forestry Commission and of private landlords include a high proportion of evergreens and this gives variety to a bleakness which might otherwise begin to pall upon the eye.

In spite of the help, financial and otherwise, given by the Crofters Commission and the Highlands and Islands Development Board, crofters in areas like this live hard. Their wives and families have to be adaptable and as the village store may be many miles away the women-folk have to be far-seeing as far as housekeeping is concerned. Every morning the children will be picked up at the road-end, possibly a fairish walk away, by the school bus and they will come home the same way in the afternoon.

In such places the country postmen carry out all kinds of errands and are as well, if not better, informed as the editor of the local newspaper about what is going on in the countryside.

In summer an increasing number of crofters are prepared to accommodate holidaymakers. They can get grants to enable them to extend their crofts for this purpose. Most crofts now are more modern than the one shown here and the old "Black House" built of turfs and roofed with thatch with a hole to let the smoke out, but windowless, is gone forever.

EILEAN DONAN CASTLE

Scattered around the coasts of Scotland are a proliferation of castles, most of them now ruined. Eilean Donan, which dates from the twelfth century was a stronghold of the MacRaes but was in grave danger of disintegrating until it was restored earlier in this century. The causeway which links it to the mainland is modern. It was originally built as a waterbound fortress and for centuries maintained its position as an impregnable stronghold until just after the first rising in favour of the Old Pretender. It was in 1719 that a force of over a thousand Highlanders with some hundred of Spanish troops under command of the Earl of Seaforth made their base at Eilean Donan and advanced to Glen Shiel where they were defeated by a larger English force. The castle surrendered after a naval bombardment. Within the reconstructed castle is a war memorial to the Clan MacRae.

THE FIVE SISTERS OF KINTAIL

Travelling westwards from Glen Moriston and continuing on the "Road to the Isles" the scenery becomes progressively more majestic. The first notable group of mountains to be seen in the "Five Sisters of Kintail". They lie in Wester Ross and when they are in sight the traveller, unless he turns back, is firmly committed to one or other of the roads to the ferries which are the only way to journey on to Skye or northwards by Strome Ferry to Torridon.

Thousands of acres of the Kintail Estate and also the Balmacara Estate now belong to the National Trust for Scotland, which means that this area will remain unspoilt in its natural state. On these estates the National Trust promotes "Adventure" holidays for young people. They help with drainage, land reclamation and forestry.

Close by are the Falls of Glomach at 370 feet, the highest in Britain. Glenelg, opposite Skye is well worth a visit but it is not possible to cross to the island by this ferry on very windy days when the race in the narrow Sound of Sleat looks like a broad river in spate.

THE CLIFFS OF SKYE

Those cliffs in Skye are a rugged reminder of the dangers that lie in wait for the unwary or the unlucky caught in boats with the wrong combination of sea and wind off the shores of many parts of the Highlands and Islands.

The classic voyage made by Flora MacDonald with Prince Charles Edward to effect his escape from the mainland to Skye was not without natural hazards being added to the energy of the pursuers. Robert Louis Stevenson gives an impressionistic, if somewhat romantic, account of what that voyage must have been like in the famous poem destined to become even better known as a song:

> *Sing me a song of a lad that has gone*
> *Say could that lad be I?*
> *Merry of soul he sailed on a day*
> *Over the sea to Skye.*

It is the memory of the Prince's wanderings and narrow escapes on the island which, quite as much as the Cuillins, brings visitors to Skye. It is an island which exerts a strong pull on the traveller, arousing hidden inner longings and satisfying them.

SLIGACHAN BRIDGE, SKYE

Sligachan Bridge, with its hotel and hostel facilities, is the focal point for climbers visiting Skye. It is the starting point for many of the best climbs in the Cuillins. There are also excellent camping grounds in Glen Sligachan. This is one of the areas in Scotland where the Aurora Borealis, the "Northern Lights", can be seen, making a majestic crown to the night sky. One of the most demanding peaks is Sgurr nan Gillian which should only be attempted by skilled climbers in peak physical condition. This is true of many of the peaks in the Black Cuillins, so called to distinguish them from the gentler Red Cuillins. It is possible for the more athletic to run up and down one of these red peaks from Sligachan and for the return trip to be timed.

Sligachan has a central position in the island. From it roads branch off east to the narrow ferry at Kyleakin or south to Ardavasar and the larger ferry across the Sound of Sleat to Mallaig. To the north one road runs to the island's capital, Portree, and continues as a circular route round the northern part of the island. To the north west another circular road passes through Glen Drynoch to Loch Harport. A turning off this road leads to Dunvegan Castle, the ancestral home of the Macleods of Skye to which members of the Clan were recently invited from all over the world to meet the present Chief, Dame Flora Macleod of Macleod.

THE VILLAGE OF TORRAN

The village of Torran lies under the shadow of the Cuillins. From land like this the crofters work extremely hard to wrest a living. The reeds keep coming up through the pasture for the cattle, but the beasts are hardily bred and thrive well on coarse grazing which more pampered beasts might reject. Oat crops are grown and also potatoes, but the soil has to be constantly weeded of stones before planting is possible.

The old economy of fishing with crofting in order to make a livelihood is fast dying out. The opportunities of getting good jobs in the Merchant Navy or on the mainland of Scotland are not to be missed by the young and adventurous. As a result many of the crofts in Skye and in other islands are kept going by the very young, the retired and womenfolk.

Tourists supplement the income and lie soft and eat hearty in many of Skye's crofts during the summer.

LUSKENTYRE SANDS

"The trouble with home", said one of the two Lewis girls on holiday in Harris, "is that it's so industrialised". Geographically Lewis and Harris together make up the Long Island. Both were part of the great Norse Empire of the eighth to twelfth centuries as their very names attest.

The action, the herring fishing, the political bustling about of the Lords of the Isles tended to be in and around Stornoway, the capital of Lewis. It still is with the herring fishing headquarters, a quick-freezing plant and a meat and oil factory sited there.

In Harris they got on with their own way of life, crofting and fishing and weaving the famous tweed which takes its name from the island.

The Harris folk were by no means to be seduced into an industrialised way of life even by the inducements offered to them by Lord Leverhulme to raise their standard of living by the efficient commercialisation of their fishing and farming activities. Leverburgh is a mute memorial to an enterprise which was kindly meant but psychologically unsound.

The broad sweep of Luskentyre Sands lies at the mouth of the river Laxdale and off-shore is the island of Taransay.

To the south of Harris are the other islands of the Outer Hebrides, North Uist, Benbecula, South Uist and Barra.

GLEN MORISTON LOOKING TOWARDS KINTAIL

Glen Moriston runs westwards from Loch Ness at first through pleasant lowland country and then it rises to join the "Road to the Isles" at Cluanie. It was through the desolate parts of this area that Prince Charles Edward was chased by the redcoats after his defeat at the Battle of Culloden.

Driven by hunger and thirst he entered a cottage, against the advice of his companions. Seven men were having a meal inside and he was instantly recognised by them. There was a reward of £30,000 on the Prince's head but the "Seven Men of Glen Moriston" swore that they would never betray him, a promise which they faithfully kept.

At Cluanie Bridge it is possible to double back to the east to Glen Garry and then along the shores of Loch Garry to Loch Oich and the Great Glen. From there the route can be taken either north through Fort Augustus with its famous school and monastery to Inverness or south to Fort William.

LOCH LAGGAN, INVERNESS-SHIRE

The scenery around Loch Laggan in Inverness-shire is further evidence of the kind of beauty that the Scottish Highlands have to offer in the winter time. But the loch is useful as well as beautiful and provides water for a hydro-electric scheme. For many years the waters of the Highlands were politically ignored as a readily available source of electrical power. Now large areas of the countryside depend on such electricity for home use and also to develop industry.

Without this power it would not have been possible to establish the Aluminium Works at Fort William or still more recently the Pulp Mill at the same centre. This mill serves a dual purpose for it can provide a handy nearby market for any suitable timber grown in the region. From the traveller's point of view it is significant that all this power can be produced without materially affecting the natural magnificence of Loch Laggan and its surroundings.

BEN NEVIS AND CORPACH

Although Ben Nevis is the highest mountain in Great Britain, its shape from Fort William is not so impressive as mountains of lesser height in other parts of the country. This is partly because Ben Nevis is not a solitary peak but pre-eminent among the surrounding mountains which are not much lower. This appearance is deceptive for it can be a dangerous mountain and offers some of the best rock climbing in Britain. It is, however, possible to climb Ben Nevis by following a track. Indeed during Victory celebrations after the Second World War, the Provost, Council, other dignitaries and athletically minded citizens climbed to the top and lit a bonfire.

It is at Corpach that the huge new pulp mill has been erected and with the Aluminium Factory this has made Fort William one of the busiest industrial towns in the Western Highlands.

It has always been the focal point for Lochaber and was indeed built as such by General Wade three centuries ago. The town commands the southern end of the Great Glen and the Caledonian Canal which run north east to Inverness. In the Great Glen and further north around Beauly successful experiments have been made in cattle ranching on a large scale. Such methods could with some encouragement and financial incentive from the powers that be bring new prosperity to vast stretches of the Highlands and produce more meat for a world in which it is always in short supply.

LOCH SHIEL

Fort William is the beginning of the last stretch of the "Road to the Isles". The route passes Glen Finnan at the top of Loch Shiel and the monument marks the spot where Prince Charles Edward raised his standard in 1745. Loch Shiel is a long inland loch and the place where the Prince first landed is some miles further on past the sea loch of Loch Ailort at Loch-nan-Uamh, a name meaning the loch of the caves. The landing took place on 5th August and some of the faithful who visit the monument leave white roses in remembrance.

At Loch Ailort there is a cairn set up by the "Forty Five Association" in 1956 with a bronze plaque commemorating the traditional spot from which Prince Charles Edward Stuart embarked for France on the 20th of September 1746.

Past Arisaig are the white "singing" sands of Morar and tremendous sunsets over Rhum and Eigg. The road ends at the fishing port of Mallaig with views of the Cuillins to the north west across the Sound of Sleat.

LOCH LINNHE, INVERNESS-SHIRE

The sunsets in the west of Scotland vary from the fiery and majestic to the most delicate shading as instanced by this study of Loch Linnhe in Inverness-shire. Across the loch are the hills of Morven and Ardnamurchan the most westerly point of the Scottish mainland. Up from the mouth of the loch stretches the long low-lying Isle of Lismore with beyond it the Firth of Lorne and the Isle of Mull.

Mull is only some thirty miles long but so indented by sea lochs that its coastline measures some three hundred miles. At the north eastern corner is Tobermory where many unsuccessful attempts have been made to locate and raise the treasure believed to have been in a Spanish galleon which foundered there after the defeat of the Spanish Armada in 1588.

Off the west coast of Mull lies the small island of Staffa with its soaring basalt pillars and Fingal's Cave.

To the south is Iona, the birthplace of Celtic Christianity in Scotland and a place of pilgrimage for visitors from all over the world, who come to see the restored cathedral and assimilate an atmosphere unique to this island which for centuries has been a holy place.

LOCH LEVEN AND GLENCOE

Loch Leven guards the seaward entrance to Glencoe. The flourishing industry at one time was slate quarrying at Ballachulish, but the quarries are now disused. From the north it is possible to reach Glencoe either by taking the ferry from north to south Ballachulish or by going the long way round through Kinlochleven at the head of the loch. The aluminium works there are now the main industrial enterprise in the area.

As such they came as a great boon to the people who live and wanted to work there, but were afraid that lack of employment would force them to leave the splendid surroundings in which they delighted. It is possible to have sympathy with the scenic purists who claim that the works at Kinlochleven spoil the grandeur of the surrounding country-side. But as far as is humanly possible they are unobtrusive, becoming increasingly so with usage, in no way disturbing the view in Glencoe, and of comparative puny significance, tucked away as they are at the head of the loch.

RAINCLOUDS OVER BEINN AIRIDH CHARR, WESTER ROSS

It would be idle, as well as palpably false, to claim that the sun always shines in the Scottish Highlands. The east coast of Scotland is drier than the west, but there is majesty in stormy weather such as this scene of rainclouds over Beinn Airidh Charr in Wester Ross.

Frequently such rain storms do not last very long and there is a hint in this study that fine weather has preceded the storm and will soon re-emerge when it has gone. One overseas visitor to the Western Highlands remarked during a spell of such weather that "It was the only place she knew in the world where it was fine five or six times a day".

The road looks and is narrow, but passing places (indicated by white posts which can be seen from a distance) are frequent and in most cases the surfaces of Highland roads are well-metalled. While it is not desirable to try to travel on these highways at speeds suitable to motorways it is possible to cover long distances comfortably in the course of a day. In any case with such scenery all around few travellers would wish to pursue their passage in a tearing hurry.

GLENCOE

Glencoe and the awful happenings there nearly three hundred years ago arouse the strongest emotions among the Scots and the thousands of visitors to the glen each year. The visitors, although welcome, create problems, not least of all hygienic; but when it was suggested that toilet facilities should be set up in the glen to alleviate the situation, there was an outburst of wrath in the correspondence columns of Scotland's national newspapers. Correspondents claimed that the site to be used was in the very spot where had stood some of the dwelling places of the Macdonalds killed in the notorious massacre of Glencoe on the night of 13th February 1692. The numbers killed were comparatively small, especially in that turbulent age. It was the manner of the killing, perpetrated as it was upon hosts by guests who had accepted for days the shelter of their homes and shared their boards, that shocked Scotland and then the world. The massacre broke a sacred, basic law of human behaviour.

Nowadays Glencoe is the happy hunting ground for hill walkers and climbers and for skiers in the winter. The Scottish national newspapers carry daily accounts of snow conditions on the slopes. But there are few who can entirely rid their minds of that earlier, bloody hunting, and it is perhaps as well for the continuance of the laws of hospitality that this should be so.

GLENORCHY

It is not much of a relief after the sombre grandeur of the Glencoe peaks, such as Buchaille Etive Mohr, the "Great Shepherd of Glen Etive" to follow the road across the wild, dank moor of Rannoch. It is more attractive in summer when the heather is out, but this would be desperate country in which to get caught without shelter in bad weather. It is a reminder of the natural dangers that men faced who had to "take to the heather" after the Fifteen and the Forty-five.

The country becomes milder on the way to Bridge of Orchy behind which is the mass of Ben Dorain celebrated in a Gaelic ode by the eighteenth-century poet Duncan Ban Macintyre.

Another notability of the district for whom an elegy in Gaelic was composed after his death in 1631 was Sir Duncan Campbell of Glen Orchy. A good landlord and a man well ahead of his times, Sir Duncan improved his estate by building roads as well as houses and churches. He also improved the breeding of horses. The original manuscript of the elegy is now in Register House in Edinburgh.

THE FALLS OF ORCHY

It is but a few miles from Bridge of Orchy to the Falls of Orchy, rushing rapids which have one or two counterparts in the Highlands. Those who love such sights and sounds will be tempted to journey on to Tyndrum where one road branches west to Loch Awe and Oban and the other south to Crianlarich and then east along Glen Dochart to the Falls of Dochart and Killin at the west end of Loch Tay.

A climb up Ben Lawers, best approached from the village of Lawers on the north bank of the loch may be exhausting but it is well worthwhile. The peak is one of the high points of a great amphitheatre looking down on an ink-black loch at the bottom. All around there are views of some of Scotland's greatest mountains stretching into the far distance.

South of Killin is Loch Earn which is within easy reach of Edinburgh and Glasgow and has become a centre for boating, canoeing, water skiing and climbing. The area around St. Fillans has a reputation for earth tremors, modest indeed, but newsworthy in a countryside noted for its unshakeability.

PERTHSHIRE LANDSCAPE

Many would agree with Sir Walter Scott that Perthshire is "the fairest portion of the Northern Kingdom". It is a land of contrast with, as shown here, rich lowland arable country rising to poorish, but charming upland slopes and then to the purple heather-clad summits of the mountains.

Through the county town of Perth the river Tay slides with a deceptive smoothness, for its swirling eddies are treacherous and have proved fatal to the unwary. It is no uncommon sight to look over one of the city's bridges and see a fisherman in thigh boots casting hopefully for salmon. The whole county is indeed a fisherman's paradise with countless smaller lochs giving added opportunities for the sport which is to be had in the great lochs of Tay and Rannoch.

On the outskirts of Perth lies Scone which was for hundreds of years the hallowed spot where the kings of Scotland were crowned. There rested the Stone of Destiny until it was carried off to England by Edward I, "the hammer of the Scots", in 1297.

Near Pitlochry with its theatre which stages plays of a high quality every summer season is Blair Castle the family seat of the Dukes of Atholl. In the nearby Pass of Killiecrankie is the "Soldier's Leap", a fantastic jump across a rugged ravine made by an English soldier fleeing from victorious Highlanders after the Battle of Killiecrankie in 1689.

SCHIEHALLION

Schiehallion is an outstanding landmark in the Perthshire countryside. No matter from which direction it is seen it impresses as a singularly handsome mountain. Its cone shape is an unusual but welcome change from the rounder aspects of many Scottish peaks. Seen by moonlight Schiehallion stands out black and with perfect grace against the sky. It is the kind of mountain which, seen first as a boy, brings back the man many times in his life.

From Loch Rannoch, a source of hydro-electricity, a pretty road winds by the River Errochty to Struan. A short walk between pinewoods, with blaeberries on the ground in season, gives a memorable view beneath of the bleached white rocks in the gorge of the river Garry. It ends in a meadow set between the meeting of the Errochty with the Garry in which stands a simple but effective country church. On a Sunday morning the singing of Scottish psalms to the traditional tunes carries across the quiet countryside and mingles with the noise of the waters in an unforgettable way.

CALLANDER

From Lochearnhead with the mass of Ben Vorlich on the right, a twisting road passes by Loch Lubnaig on the west and enters the narrow Pass of Leny with its spectacular waterfall and so into Callander and the Lowlands. It is a sudden transition from rugged to gentle and fertile country. The Lowland landscape takes on subtleties of colour which were perhaps too much taken for granted before the traveller passed through the Highlands. Regrettably after a while the memories of the Highland scene slide into a dream world as if the journey had never been made. The remedy is to go back to see if the eyes have been deceived, and this process can almost achieve a lifelong state of perpetual motion.

Callander is a notable touring centre well supplied with hotels. Fourteen miles away lies Stirling with an ancient castle on a precipitous rock. It was among other objectives to ensure the surrender of this key stronghold between the north and south of Scotland that Robert the Bruce fought and won the Battle of Bannockburn in 1314. At Stirling there is a nineteenth-century monument to William Wallace, Bruce's less fortunate predecessor, on Abbey's Craig just outside the town.

LOCH KATRINE AND THE TROSSACHS

The Trossachs lie just west of Callander and it is entirely possible for overseas visitors to take a quick run round them in a day and imagine that they have covered the Scottish Highlands. The Trossachs are pretty enough, but as far as Highland country is concerned, they spell out little more than a beginner's primer compared with the epic language revealed by the true Highland country to the north.

The inflated reputation of the area is due above all to Sir Walter Scott and in particular the adventures related in *Rob Roy* and *The Lady of the Lake*. Even before Scott, the Wordsworths were in on the act. No countryside in Britain could hope to survive unspoilt the combined approbation of those poets, unless it were so remote as to be well out of reach of transport powered by the internal combustion engine. Loch Vennachar, Loch Katrine and the rest are well worth a visit for they are beautifully set in charming countryside. The wise, however, make the pilgrimage in early spring or late autumn and there is much to be said for holding out for a crisp, sunny winter's day.

LOCH LOMOND

The song is right. The Banks of Loch Lomond are "bonny", but it is inadvisable to try to motor slowly round on a summer's day in competition with coaches, caravans on tow, commercial trucks and speeding youngsters on motor cycles.

It is far better to put the car away and walk along the shores of the loch or, if you prefer, to take passage on one of the steamers like the *Maid of the Loch* and spend a day cruising up and down among the islands and islets of this twenty-one mile long freshwater highway. If the weather is fine there is much to be said for the looks of the "steep steep sides of Ben Lomond".

At Inversnaid the English Government stationed a garrison during the troubled times of the first half of the eighteenth century. Its special task was to end the activities of Rob Roy and presumably the man himself. This must have been an unpopular posting, with the garrison's faces frequently as red as their tunics as time after time Rob Roy slipped through their fingers by the narrowest of margins and was never successfully held.

For many years after Rob Roy's death the garrison was maintained at Inversnaid presumably to catch his ghost if it dared to rise from his reputed grave at the Braes of Balquhidder.

LOCH AWE

Citizens of the United States are apt to suspect that their legs are being pulled when they are told that New York stands on the banks of Loch Awe in Argyll. Yet it is so, although the settlement so named is scarcely even a hamlet.

Ben Cruachan, a massive guardian at the foot of the loch, is honeycombed with tunnels and contains within itself a huge hydro-electric power station. The only external signs of this are the white dam high on the mountainside and some minor workings in the Pass of Brander.

There are many attractive islets in this loch and at its head is Kilchurn Castle, a Campbell stronghold built in the mid-fifteenth century.

The Highland cattle shown in the picture are to be found all over the Western Islands and are useful as well as picturesque. When they are crossed with the Scotch Beef Shorthorns and other breeds they produce meat very thriftily, in keeping with the Scottish character.

THE CRINAN CANAL

The basin at the Crinan end of the Crinan Canal is half-empty and was obviously photographed on a calm day. Had it been during a summer storm or its aftermath the basin would have been so filled with fishing boats and pleasure craft that it would have been simple to walk across it dry-shod. In the far background are the outlines of the mountains of Mull.

The Crinan Canal winds through the narrow neck of the peninsula to Ardrishaig on Loch Fyne. From Ardrishaig there is a spectacular run south to Tarbert and then down the wild Atlantic coast of the peninsula of Kintyre with views of the islands of Jura, Islay and Gigha, to the port of Campbeltown. This round trip continues up the milder wooded east coast of Kintyre, past Carradale, with views all along of the west coast of Arran in the Clyde estuary and of that island's mountains. And so back to the main road to the north near Whitehouse.

INVERARAY CASTLE

Inveraray Castle and the town of Inveraray itself were built by the Duke of Argyll in the eighteenth century. Before that time Inveraray was a fishing village with little or no pretentions to style. The eighteenth-century buildings of today, gaily painted in a style reminiscent of the Mediterranean, look especially delightful on a bright sunny day from the opposite side of Loch Fyne when their reflection as well may be seen etched sharply in the clear water.

The castle on the outside of the town was designed by Robert Morris and William Adam. Much of the interior decoration was planned by Robert Mylne. The building was finished at the beginning of the 1780s. There are family portraits, some by famous Scottish artists like Ramsay and Raeburn. The castle also boasts a veritable arsenal of broadswords, claymores, dirks and other offensive weapons.

In the springtime, with quite as pugnacious a spirit, the local youth engage in shinty matches in the castle grounds. Shinty is the more lethal brand of hockey played in the Scottish highlands. Mixed shinty is unheard of and best unthought of.

DUNDERAVE CASTLE

Of considerably older construction than Inveraray Castle is Dunderave Castle with a commanding position on a small promontory jutting out into Loch Fyne. It is a classic example of a house built equally for defence and domestic amenity. It was erected by the Chief of the Macnaughtons in the late sixteenth century, so strongly that although its walls bear the marks of roundshot it did not, like so many of its contemporaries, fall into ruins.

In the early part of the twentieth century, it is true, that it was for a time without a roof; but the whole house was restored just before the First World War by Sir Robert Lorimer who was later the architect responsible for the design of the National Shrine for the war dead in Edinburgh Castle.

Approaching from Glasgow after the barren stretches of Glenfinlas the shores of Loch Fyne are a pleasant wooded contrast, sporting oaks and shrubs, like rhododendrons, in liberal quantities.

LOCH ECK

Loch Eck and Loch Lomond are the only inland lochs in Scotland to produce fresh water herrings. These are called "Powens" and are almost identical with herring from the sea except of course that they do not have a salty flavour. South from Loch Eck is the Holy Loch now a base for Polaris submarines.

Loch Eck is less frequently visited than the nearby and more famous Loch Lomond, but it is well worth seeing for its own sake and because, past it, the road leads on to Dunoon, Inellan, Rothesay and other Clyde resorts and also to the Kyles of Bute. The most effective way of appreciating this countryside is to see it from one of the steamers plying in the Clyde estuary. It can be quite a gay experience in the summer with the band playing lively Scottish and other airs. In the middle of the Clyde lies the island of Arran with an impressive chain of mountains including the highest Goat Fell and the group known from its shape as the Sleeping Warrior. It is countryside suited both to the hill walker and the rock climber. There are two sea-angling festivals a year in Arran, at Lamlash in the spring and at Brodick in the autumn. Brodick Castle has a walled rose garden dating from 1710 and a notable collection of huge-bloomed rhododendrons.

GIRVAN

Girvan and the Ayrshire coast have long been a holiday playground for Scotland and particularly for Glasgow and industrial Lanarkshire. Girvan has a sporting golf course of its own and is not far from the renowned links at Turnberry. It is still a considerable fishing port, for herring are to be caught in the Clyde estuary almost all the year round and not for a short season as in most parts of Scotland. Girvan has too an active boat-building industry with surprising international connections; for an astonishing variety of wood is needed to build these boats. They incorporate oak from Scotland, Oregon pine from U.S.A., white pine from Sweden and the Soviet Union as well as teak from Burmah and mahogany from West Africa.

Fishing is a serious business, but a lighter hearted form of sailing is a pleasure cruise round Ailsa Craig, the large granite rock ten miles to the west. It is famous for its lighthouse, its seabirds, the occasional eagle and for its granite from which are fashioned curling stones for use by devotees of the "Roarin' Game" throughout the world.

THE MULL OF GALLOWAY

The road from Girvan to the Mull of Galloway runs along a wild rocky seacoast with views of the peninsula of Kintyre and the Irish coast. It passes through a famous early potato-growing district near Ballantrae which gave its name to R. L. Stevenson's novel *The Master of Ballantrae,* despite the fact that the action was actually set around Borgue near Kirkcudbright. At the head of Loch Ryan is Stranraer from which steamers sail to Northern Ireland.

At Logan House there are beautiful sub-tropical gardens and at Port Logan a pool built at the time of the Napoleonic Wars. In this were kept cod which became so tame that they could be hand fed. There are still cod there, some of them of enormous size.

The rocky headland of the Mull and the moorland grazing on the top are in sharp contrast to the lush wooded farmland of the Galloway countryside around Glenluce and Newtonstewart.

It was of this part of the world that Thomas Carlyle observed: "There is no finer or more beautiful drive in the Kingdom than the one round the shore of the Stewartry by Gatehouse-of-Fleet". When Queen Victoria asked John Ruskin for his views on Galloway he could do no better than quote Carlyle.

KIRKCUDBRIGHTSHIRE

Kirkcudbrightshire is famous livestock country, particularly for the hardy Galloway and Belted Galloway beef breeds and also for the red-and-white Ayrshire dairy herds. It is also steeped in Scottish history. Robert Burns is believed to have composed "Scots wa' hae" while he was walking across the hills from Lauriston to Gatehouse-of-Fleet: appropriately enough, for it was in this area that Robert the Bruce began his long campaign to achieve the independence of Scotland from England.

The spirit of an independent way of life is still preserved in Galloway, which is maybe why the region is so popular with artists and writers. One man of independent mind who was born at Arbigland was John Paul Jones, the founder of the American Navy. While this is largely a country of rolling hills, woods and streams, there are coastal inlets perfect for sailing and swimming. On the higher hills is the Glentrool National Forest Park.

The whole area is rich in early archaeological sites of before and after Pictish times. The thirteenth-century triangular castle of Caerlaverock on the marshy Solway Firth in Dumfriesshire was sacked by Edward the First in 1300 but rebuilt in the fifteenth century. Now it is again, after many vicissitudes, ruined, but the ruins are well preserved by the Ministry of Works.

DUMFRIES

Dumfries is a busy market town where tweed and wool are produced. One of its great sights is when the Solway rushes up the narrowing mouth of the estuary at full tide to meet the downward flow of the river Nith. The Solway is indeed a treacherous firth and the salmon spearing made famous by Sir Walter Scott in *Redgauntlet* was a most hazardous occupation.

Robert Burns lived and worked here as an Excise Officer, patronised many of the local taverns and is buried with Jean Armour under a mausoleum of controversial taste in St. Michael's churchyard.

The Observatory Museum has a very fine and well-presented collection of display pieces connected with the surrounding countryside, as well as a fascinating "camera obscura".

From many points outside Dumfries the English traveller, sated with things Scottish, can see the welcoming hills of the Lake District. It is only a short thirty miles to Carlisle with a passing glance at Gretna Green, always remembering that runaway anvil marriages at the Smiddy there are no longer legal.

Acknowledgment

The Publishers wish to thank the following for permission to reproduce photographs appearing in the book:

G. Douglas Bolton, for pages 41, 75, 101 and 105; J. Allan Cash, for pages 25, 31, 63 and 107; V. K. Guy, for pages 49 and 55; Noel Habgood, for pages 19-23, 27, 37, 39, 43, 47, 51, 53, 57-61, 67-73, 77-81, 85, 87, 93-97, 103, 109, 111; A. F. Kersting, for pages 29, 33 and 35; Kenneth Scowen, for pages 17, 45, 65, 89, 91 and 99; Fred. G. Sykes, for page 83.